The Space
Between
Spark and Flame

The Space
Between
Spark and Flame

The Poetry of Maria and Matt Hawn

Illustrated by Maria Hawn

The Space Between Spark and Flame

First Printing: 2020

ISBN: 978-1-73458-110-2

Maria and Matt Hawn
1070 Jefferson Street
Saint Charles, MO 63301

To Canyon,

May the expression of your heart be trusty and true

Part I: Equinox

Hesitation

Hesitation.
The space between spark and flame.

Hesitation.

Will my words communicate? Or lose
the very essence of the expression:
the resonance of creation
within my confession.

Walking.
Walking.
Walking.
And then I catch it.
The initial attention to the sounds around me.
Shh...

I softly silence my lover,
pausing to attention.
Attention that delivers,
a covering of nature's medicine.

The noises around my mind,
body vibrations and inner anxiety,
all fall to the dirt marked road under my feet.
The ears and eyes of my heart perk up enlightened.
Encapsulated by the tranquil chaos of hundreds of distinct noises
all colliding together around me.

Around me.
Can it be they call to me?
Listen! Listen! To what the earth is saying.
Heart alert, mind calm, body longing;
attuning to sound.
Splicing through the orchestra to hear each particular creature express its
note.

Oh wait, it's me!
I am a glorious sound expressed in creation!

Hearing my awakening in the unspoken,
The crowd of creatures quiet themselves.

Listen, I say to my lover.
They have paused.

Can it be?
They long to hear from you and me?

Just as I have longed for their sounds
to resonate through my inner being.
They still themselves
awaiting to receive.

Hesitation.

Can it be?

The song bird does not hesitate whistling its tune tightly.
The tree frog does not hesitate croaking its nightfall covering.
The cricket does not hesitate playing its calling cordially.
The goose does not hesitate squawking its invitation intently.
The wind does not hesitate blowing in whooshing wildly.

Simple, simple, I am craving this simply.
Let it be unto me.
No hesitation in the space between.

The Secret Garden

A seed below,
Awaiting production.
It's time to show,
Nature's reflection.
What's been hidden, untold,
The story expresses.
Each seedling undresses.
Bursting forth
The secret revealed once more.

A New Sense

Mother, Mother, are you there?
Your silence is deafening.

Or is it that my ears do not yet understand?
Your voice does not compute
in this current of machine language.
Like a newborn I know you are here.
I feel your presence.
Yet your sound, your messages,
Are a language I am only beginning to understand.
When the sun and moon rise and fall
What does this mean? What does this speak?
A language foreign to me? To the machine?
Is that what I am?
My eyes and ears have been conditioned
through binary codes of downloads and data,
That the voice of the wind
I can only contend
        Will take time to adjust from distant to within.

Like a newborn I trust, awaiting your reply,
Growing into newness with every blink of my eyes.
They are tired; adjusting to this new sight.
The weariness of the in between speaks,
"I am ok, all is alright."
These are the natural adjustments
that I always ignored,
When I thought I was machine,
before I knew more.

More than my body and mind could conceive,
in this present moment no space to believe.
Only accept and receive
What is happening to me.
All along I am pleased.
Awakening my soul to be.

Opened, evolving, listening.
Mother, Mother, I hear thee.

Remember

Tenderness of the ground below
inviting my feet to rest.
Wholly sinking in
a bodily embrace
for this dis-integrated one.
With each step I remember:
safety, connection, intimacy.
Communion with Divine Creator.
I am a part of the whole.

The buzzing chaos of the city I left behind
continues traveling from my head through each nerve in my body
releasing down through my toes into the muddy embrace.
I am not of that.
I am of this.
Dust to Dust,
I remember.
While in this tenderness.

Untitled

Another brick in the wall
crumbles down.
As I peak through
looking to the other side,
again the view has changed.
A wall begins to crumble.
Stones that held together something
good are breaking.
Shattering mindsets, frameworks,
doctrines of desperation, separation and condemnation of other.
Without bending, adjusting, or adapting to new,
one crashes down with the rubble.
Frantic and panicked with fear,
the rebuild begins from old floor plans.
Crash. Rip. Swoop. There goes the rug.
Who is there to catch you
when you fall from this tower that you built?
Pulling together the walls of protection;
boundaries you have built in fear.
You are free. Do you not know?
You are the Temple.
Why are you building upon shaky ground?

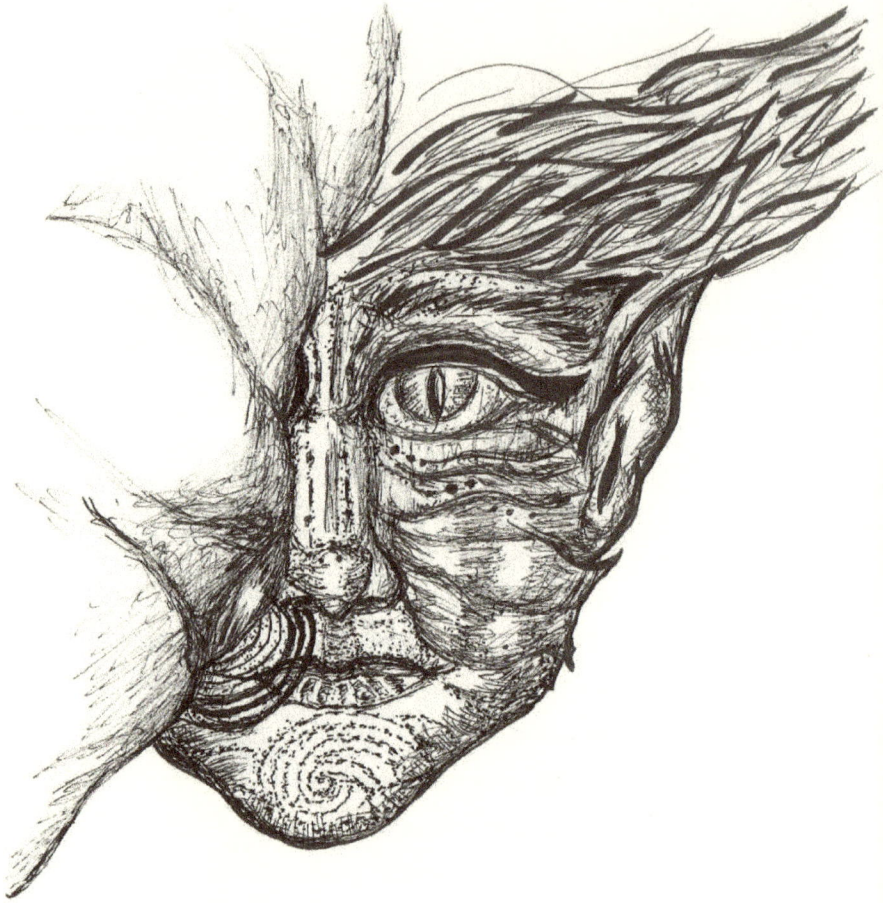

Lost in Discovery

On the playground I sat
Lost in Discovery
Time stood still in space

I found a stone
With intricate detail
Detail that felt infinite and immeasurable

Yet nestled into my tiny hand
When I held it to my heart
I could feel it beat
It felt near
When I looked with my eyes
The forms took shape
A whole world embedded into the rock face
Tuning my ears I could hear chatter
From a people, a place
 In a language I could not trace
Yet I felt a familiar embrace
A people together
With belonging in their voices and invitation to commune
Open to being discovered as my heart attunes

The Heron

Precise
Intention
Gracious
Placement
Unmoved
Unwavered
Outward Pathways
Consciously
Kept at Bay
Accuracy Aligned
Steadied Intention
Meeting
Within
Uninfluenced
Decision
Confidently
The Heron Takes Flight

The Storm

The motherless ones wait in the cold dark night
   hoping for a storm;
   something to keep them company.
The storm sounds close.
The smell of the rain activates memories of together.
Lightning strikes bright, illuminating sight.
Thunder rumbles, echoing inside the body resembling touch.

The uncertainty of the storm is familiar
   and comforting to the motherless ones.
"Thank you storm for being alive!", we cry.
The taste of grateful tears bring life into the cold dark night.

The Dance of the Intimate Divine

In the silence of the soul
The king comes in.
Arriving with praise.
Arriving with grief.
Knocking upon the door of the inner chambers.

Beholding the answer she stands tall.
Opening the door the invitation is clear,
"Come in, come closer, lay down fear."
Inside you find all that you seek
And all that has been seeking you will find.

Pausing, eyes meet.
Beholding.
Beheld.
Her reaching arms fall away,
Unleashing his armor, embrace and dismay.
Eyes meeting;
The melting of two souls.
Standing firm they surrender
In love's fiery folds.
Unique ones they remain,
Eyes locked and infinitely intertwined,
In this dance of the intimate divine.

I AM

Go There!
Where?
To the deep!
Drift, Dive, Explore, Rise.
Into, under, through;
the depths and layers.

Breathe in life.
Delight in all.

Drift, Dive, Explore, Rise.
Waves crash on the shore above.
And still I become.
Floating below.
Letting go.

Amongst the deep sea mysteries
I breathe in by your breath,
I look out by your light,
I hear through your expression,
"I AM"
spoken in and through all of creation.
A resounding collective response from deep within,
"Glory, Glory, Alleluia. Amen."

Today I Kissed a Giraffe

I kissed a giraffe and it made me giggle;
its tongue was long and fickle.
I had no idea the kiss would tickle.
This one was gentle and slobbered less than the last.
Boy or girl, I don't know, I didn't think to ask!

Mushroom, Mushroom

The mushrooms are calling, "Open up to me!
And you will you see
Euphoria, wellness, openness and clarity.
The magic we hold is one to be shared.
Invite us, ingest us, when you are ready to care.
We invite you to partake, enjoy and proceed.
Learning and waiting patiently,
To see all that is in store for humanity.

"We have known you for years,
Millions to be clear.
Through the ebbs and flows of natural rhythm.
Species come and go, but only few will listen.
We are the body's ancient teacher,
patiently waiting for every creature.
To unfold.
Unfolding within connection,
Free from mind body deception.
We meet each soul in its own silence,
One meeting All in sovereign alliance.

"You must see past the ordinary;
Ordinary grids of man made systems.
Crawling and creeping with parasitic inventions.
Intentions unknown to the maker,
Driven by a source that is not their own,
An external influence begging to take a home.
Sweeping out recollection of the space within and in between.
All of creation crying out to be seen."

Man or machine,
What will it be?
Will we continue forgetting,
The infinince of our design and chemistry?

Listen, listen, intently and you will see,
All that is waiting your discovery.

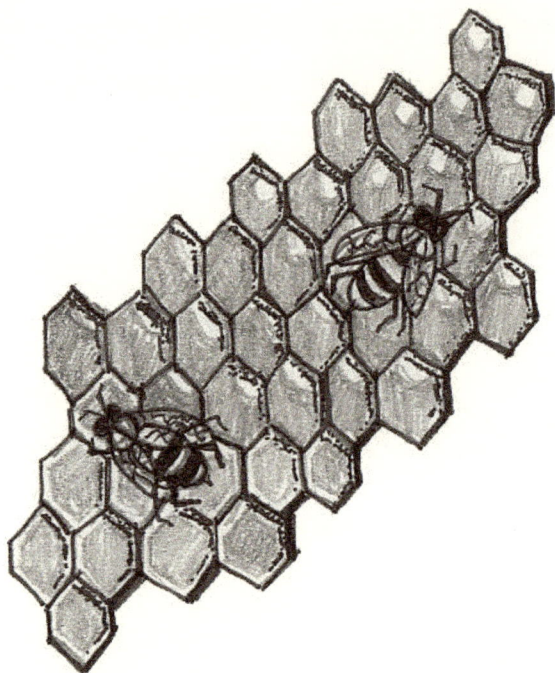

A Queenless Hive

Observing bees in a queenless hive

Working and waiting, directionless until a queen arrives.

Like explorers navigating by stars on a cloudy night

They await the sunrise or the next clear view.

Until then, the ocean carries them through.

As the observer of your own life

If you are viewing your self as lost,

You are not what is lost.

If you are waiting for the stars to guide you,

You are neither the one who waits nor the stars.

All are a part of the whole,

But all that you observe is not who you are.

A queen is birthed and takes her throne.

With awareness of her presence,

Purpose and guidance have come home.

The bees are working just as busy as before.

One thing has changed they are directionless no more.

Talitha Koum

There she goes again,
a knife to the heart.
Stabbing.
Piercing.
Wounding the very instrument
that is outpouring love.
Self hatred;
cutting in order to bleed out.
Quickly.
Swiftly.
Without relent.
Wanting to prevent
another from beating her to the pain.
Before the knife can come
from any of those
she pours love upon,
she twists the blade into her heart. Protecting from
the foreseen yet only remembered
pain of rejection.
Manipulation.
Deception.
The twisting of love so near to fear
she sits again aching.
Fearing that the very love
overflowing from her, to heal
people, lands, and nations,
will still be used against her.
Perpetuating the pain and misery
of the young one,
who at one time only knew pure love.
Freely giving, freely receiving,
over time,
over pain.
She closed up from the very source

of love, light, and hope she longed for.

Yet she is awakened.
Waking.
Woke.
Not dead only sleeping
Talitha koum!

Gently she places one hand over the other.
Together they remove the knife,
unpiercing her own heart.
She lays down the weapon at the feet of
the One who was pierced for all transgressions.
Wounded by knife;
taking upon himself all the pain.
With open hands she weeps at his feet,
holding arms outstretched in hopes of reception.

In faith he pours upon her hands
a living water, basked with sweet aroma,
A savory balm, warm and gentle.
She places her hands, full of grace, upon her own heart.
Mending the wounds.
Breathing in sweetness.
Wrapped in kindness.
Her heart is restored.
Like new wine,
a rich, full, embodied love flows.
Drinking in deeply.
Pouring out freely.
Resting.
Rest.
Restored you are
my sweet little girl.

The Kingdom has Come

Labor in Vain or Glory abounding?
Do we toil til no end?
Waiting our wages to amend?
Passing each day
Without a trace of pay.
Did we miss the trade?
Or were the glory and wages already paid?

32

Cotopaxi

Broccoli, carrots, cabbage, and beets,
oh my, what a glorious treat!
Free to grow, free to be, free to eat.
All in rows tidy and neat.
Walking, admiring, gathering
in my bare feet.

The ground is rich, the air is bright.
The rooster crows at first light.
Awakening all in ears distance
to greet the day with least resistance.
Growing, flourishing, dreaming, communing,
planted, rooted, hoping, resting.
All at the feet of the majestic one.

Boldly beaming, our eyes anticipate,
as the light illumines its form.
The clouds part, the fog dissipates,
majesty revealed, its presence adorns.

One by one in order and grace
they each ascend to gather in place.
High, o high, they come together.
All tribes, all tongues, one heart forever.
Overseers, they stand in humility and reverence.
Hand in hand passing the pipe of peace.
Holding firm, united in place.
Uniquely reflecting every other face.
Losing touch with all that is no longer

serving the good of the higher power.
In hope of love, in response to grace,
in honor of mercy, we stand, we embrace.
Calling out for surrender and release,
Open up to be, one humanity.

Broccoli, carrots, cabbage and beets,
oh my, what a glorious treat!

Tenderhearted I

To brush against the flesh of another
with only the slightest impression.
Feeling floods in, a sea of emotion.
A piece released, a heart whole no longer.

To brush against the flesh of another.
Partaking in the subtle exchange
of you, of me, of them, of we.
The tenderhearted embrace,
partake and release,
In the dance within
and in between,
flesh, spirit, heart and mind.
All to be Humankind.

Tenderhearted II

Beware ye tenderhearted.
To hear the water rush past without stopping,
To feel the wind gust through without asking,
Makes ye tenderhearted, open to bear
The uncertainty, the weight, the deep moves of the spirit.
Unable to grasp it, unable to contain.
The tenderhearted remain,
Grasping what cannot be constrained.

Beware ye tenderhearted.
Like a subtle sound that stimulates the eardrum,
The tendered heart is brushed with moving waves of love.
Ebbing and flowing, rising and crashing,
The tenderheart deepens.

Deep.
Deepening.
Depths.

Arising and resurfacing,
Returning to taste once again.
The gentleness of the morning dew kiss.
The warmth of the dawning sun's embrace.
The sweetness of a brush with genuine love.
Fear flutters away
And the tender heart opens again.

Grief is a Medicine

It is our tenderness that makes us strong and flexible.
Moving in and through this humanity adapting.
Grieving, grieving, grieving, out of old and into new.

Grief is a medicine tending to
the infinite layers of dimensional living that are shed,
in seasons,
in moments,
in lifetimes.

Grief is the portal
to which ashes become beauty,
to which old branches become ripe with healing fruit.
Grief is the portal
to which death becomes new life,
to which "who told you you were naked" becomes naked and unashamed.

I have always known you and you have always known me.
Grief is the access in which we have been gifted,
to remember,
to rediscover,
to uncover.

Grief is the salve smoothed over blind eyes
Opened to receive second sight.
To revive what has always been
yet is now new to the receiver.

Tender is the malleable vessel
Moving through grief.
Receiving new heart,
new eyes,
new lives.

The Womb

It is in this place of mercy and grace
that love flows through.
Encased, we are faced
with nothing more, nothing less, than rest.

Divine arriving in,
flowing through
without trace of the giver,
without inquiry of payment,
without cost of recompense.

Intricately woven with only
the light of the eyes to see.
In the darkness one's clearest reflection
is illuminated by one's own sight.
Created intentionally,
receiving form from beyond our control.
Yet intimately intertwined
with all that is,
all that was,
and all that will ever be.

Beheld.
Beholding.
Creation in womb.
Beginning in rest,
we end in rest.
What of the in between?
Shall we enter back into the womb?

The invitation has been sent
in divine flesh. Welcoming all
to release,
into Eternal Rest.

The Wind

The wind in me
Me in the wind
Only to remember
What has always been
A breath a movement
In leaf on tree
Roots secure
In life below
Swaying bending
In ease and flow
The tickling tenderness
Of its nurturing speech
Only heard
Only received
In my heart so deep
Letting go
Mind sleeps
Sleeping sleeping
Wind sweeping
Across tree into me
Leaf by leaf
A cleansing sweep
Uncovering heart
With each cool breeze
Opening I hear
The message more clear
Opening I long
For more my dear
Sweet tree

You are a gift to me
If only I pause
Pause to open
This gentle breeze
Becomes life in me

44

Collage

Heavens Above
Roots Below
Secrets of the garden
Only the devoted know

A glass of new wine
Invites all to dream
Exploring and creating
The space within and between

With eyes covered
All will discover
What only hearts have seen

Eternal Patience of the Mother

Always holding a warm embrace,
with open arms and room to play.
Never a judgement of where or who.
Accepting love within and through.
Afloat a river.
Below the sea.
Atop a mountain.
In a cool breeze.
Always waiting for her children to return.
Open she receives.
Forever our home.

3 Little Birds

Catching a ride on the river's flow.
Perched on a log, no worries, afloat.
Sitting cozy together with no place to go.
Little birds, rest free and whistle your note.

Tears of the Saints

The tears of the saints fall to the ground
quenching the thirst of the parched land,
the dried up seed,
and every new sprout.
The tears of the saints are holy, glory filled droplets.
No one can steal them.
No one can stop them.
They refresh the soil, the soul and the harvest.
The tears are the hope that restoration is coming,
and newness is on the horizon.
The tears of the saints do not go to waste.
They are not forgotten or ignored.
They are collected and adored,
transforming this world.
The New Heavens and New Earth proclaim,
"Weary saints, your tears are not shed in vain."

Home

The coming and going, connecting of soul, is taking a toll on my human existence.
This body aches from the pain.
Here and now nowhere to go.
There and then nowhere to be.
Together is allusive,
never guaranteed, never permanent.
My psyche is stretched with ways to forget the intimate connection that is and will always be. An undercurrent flowing through but never stopping.
No one and no thing to grasp.

What will come of all the coming and going?
The constant shifting; sharing of Home to empty space.
The distance is perception: time, space, energy, awareness, feeling, desire, longing.
All this gets stretched, pulling from what once was Home.
What is this aching in my bones?
Home shifting?
Home stretching?
Home collapsing?
Breaking down what was built up to hold space for another soul?

This Home is closed. No more may enter.
No room in the Inn. Under construction forever.

The world was tired of all the blood shed,
  the death, loss, heartache and uncertainty.
  The Inn was full.
"Make way for the King!" One would yell.

Closing their doors, each had had enough of kingship in their time.
But this feels different, could this King be new.
"Make way, make room!" The prophet proclaims.
The people are hurting and unable to hear the sound of what is coming.
It does not pierce through the noise;
the grotesque voices of their own pain have drowned them in sorrow.
The Prophet shouts louder "Make way for the King!"

They all fall sleeping.
Too much to bear with what they have been through.
Their souls are weary and sleep is their only sedative.
They awake to a faint cry, a baby in the distance.
The sound echoes throughout space, time and place.
The cry meets all.
Resonating through every chamber of the heart
their cry is met with that of a babe.
A way to connect the perception: time, space, energy, awareness, feeling,
desire, longing.

This same cry precedes and joins another.
The babe who's name proclaims,
 "God with us"
grows into a man whose cry at death exclaims,
"My God, my God why have you forsaken me?"
Reverberating back and forth the cries grow louder,
echoing in my own heart and head.

What is one to do?
What is one to be
in the echo of these two cries?
Together. With.

Forsaken. Left.
Elated sensations of always being known, never alone.
Tortuous agony of separation into the unknown.
Cries echo.
Body remembers.
Birth into existence.
Death out of life.
Soul remembers.
"It is finished."
And Life begins again.

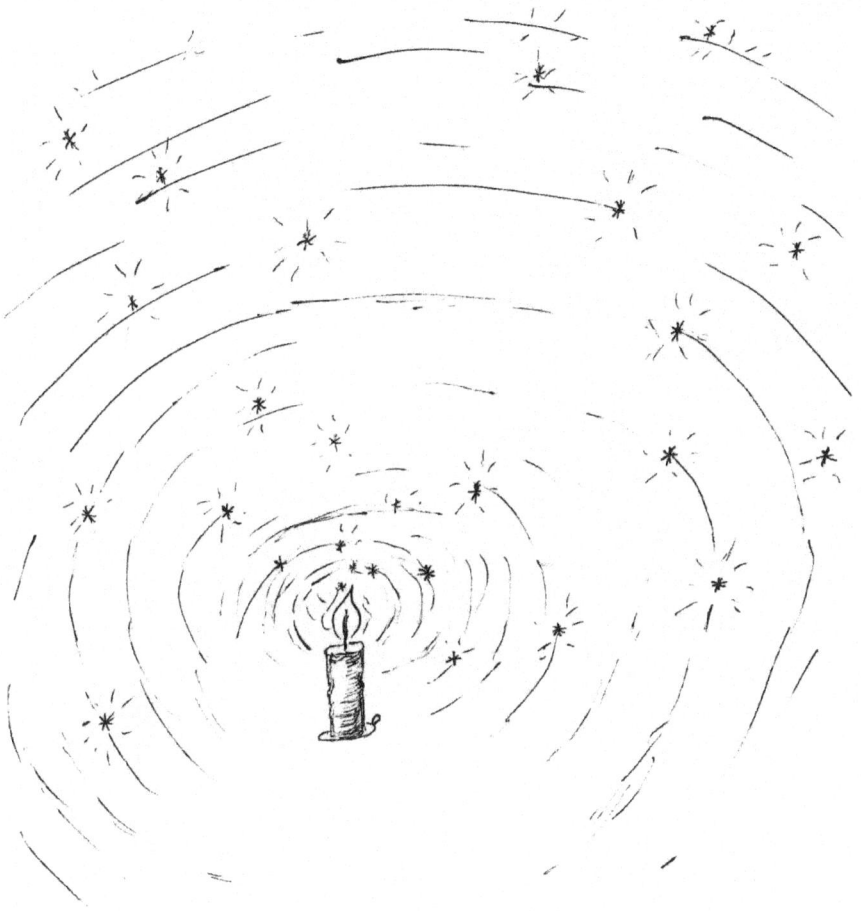

Night Fall

When night falls and daylight dwells far;
I will stand;
I will sleep.
I will fall into what I do not see.
In hope, I feel in light unseen.
I dream without holding in frame
the darkness of space in front of me.
With a glimpse I will perceive,
with a sight gifted unto me.
Loosely grasping this reality.

I fly above.
I sink below.
The cosmos hold the most ancient of souls.
The seas encompass treasures untold.
Reaching high.
Unfolding low.
Pleasantly between.
Presently free.
The night holds a hope
that need not be seen.

In the Garden

Oh Masculine Divine,
Your order in chaos is tasty and sweet
Lining edges and borders measured feet by feet
Precision and accuracy are your fine tuned skills
You speak and create action packed thrills
The seeds you plant inspire and remain
Rooted we grow in the garden just the same

Oh Feminine Divine,
Your chaos in order is glorious and delicious
Swirling whimsically around spiritually ambitious
Nurturing and wildcraft are your inheritance
You dream and envision abundant worlds of dependence
The wisdom you water clears and sustains
Rooted we grow in the garden just the same

Part II: Solstice

Silence

As I walk amid the broken
            Land, I am met by silence.
It is a silence beyond one sense;
            As felt clinging to the skin,
As peering into a morning fog so dense.

It is a silence not of rest
            Nor peace, but desolation.
The earth profaned in to exhaustion,
            Hidden and full of fear lest
I am an'ther returned for consumption.

I move south in to a bare field.
            Once ordained with dogwood beauty,
Leaf and flower in melody.
            Only stumps remain, concealed
By a choking stillness, weeds and ivies.

Turning to move on I notice
            Her fleeing where she just lay.
A single doe, bounding away
            Quietly, without malice.
Yet I know her action condemns my ways.

I kneel down on the hard, worn trail;
               Looking around at all that
Man has taken. This land once sat
               Unadultered; love unveiled.
I kneel, feeling hopeless, in broken plat.
                   Tears well up in my eyes, spilling
                   Forth, piercing the silent air.
                   Offering a repentant prayer.

Through the silence, sounds begin refilling;
A warm rain is falling, its song is shared.

A Daily Death

I am experiencing a death that is so near
To life it would fool
The most astute physician.
It is a daily dying, over
And over and over throughout each day,
Beginning deep within.
Beyond the physical alone (although
Not excluding); past a pulse,
Temperature or function.
What good is death if
It must be relived and sunk
Further in to day after day.
The gift of finality
Seems so far away
As I am reminded again
To die,
(Damn my own heart and mind).

Holy Ground

This land with earth, with water,
With plant, with animal, with man.
It is a source, no, the source,
Of life, of warmth, of awe. Amen.

And yet in all its majesty
The land demands not worship of beings.
It asks and invites only to be
Humble and grateful, with hearts for seeing.

The land belongs not to man, and we
Belong not fully to the land. However
Together we belong to each
Other. Each to care and be cared for.

With weak and quiet hearts we may
Hear the land shout forth in prophetic rage.
Both judging man and extending grace.
Pleading for a change of way.

In every way we must remember
Glory is near at hand. A willing
Vessel awaits out of enclosure
With love forgiving and receiving.

Numb

The suppressive cold numbs my total being,
Burrowing neath outer layer into cardiactric depths.
Seeking to make a home where it is not welcome,
The engulfing cold steals homely warmth and breath.

"You are not welcome here!" I scream
With fist clenched, shoulders tight, stinging tears in my eyes.
"I know of the heat, the warmth, and the life;
The ease and smiles of sun-filled skies."

And yet you remain, invasive cold; a refugee
In a land you do not belong and may never leave.
You have fled from a place of violence and hurt,
And now, o consuming cold, to my heart, why must you cleave!?

Must you sting so bitterly!?
Must you invade all spaces so violently!?
Must you devour commotion so intently!?
Must you depress life so completely!

Oh be gone! You forsaken, wretched devil,
Free myself from your agonizing grasp!

Oh how I long for my grandfather's cabin,
Fire dancing under mantle, grandma's warmth, peace, safety.

I Enter the Woods

I enter the woods on my own accord,
Seemingly.
With a notion to take, take what is given, store;
An identity.
Pressing forth, taking aim, all in;
Sought victory.
Based on success, consumption,
Submissivity.
All has been given, gifted, gotten, so get!
Take! Subdue!
Is this not what man was made for?
An endless tune
Of search, scour, stomp, trod, tear, power.
Look what man can do!
Having been given an image, I forget
What is true.

I now sit, silent and stifled, in the stillness
Of defeated success.
My accord has been softened, my feet slowed,
My mind stilled.
What was meant to be took has now taken
Me back; awakened.
Invited me into an eternal echo of
Life, death, harmony.
My part in this song is a simple one,
A flesh and soul audience

Entering into intermission, selah,
The Standing Seventh Sunrise.
Here all that is to be taken is a part
In the mystery
Of love and grace.
A gift given for all eternity.

The Nights New Snow

To awaken to the nights new snow
Resting upon house, tree, and field,
Brings peace amidst stillness.
Arising from darkness' anxieties into
A new world blanketed white, and light,
Is an invitation to re-exist.

Then there is the joyous descent from
Simply seeing to beholding the
Divine work of the sky.
Stepping out of the confinement spaces
That sustain life; entering the brisk
Unknown, seeking to flourish, to thrive.

The nights new snow reminds me
For freedom I've been set free.
Return not to slavery.
Go forth into jubilee!

A Sacred Space

Sitting stillness, steel in hand; lived contradiction.
Restless, weighty, lead,
All around, life abounds; lived glory's depiction.
Hidden heights, dread,
Beast and bird, their lives observed; glad benediction.
Man, misled,
Is this place, a sacred space; freedom from affliction?
Blood shed,
Life-full fawn, steal the dawn; Receive my confliction!
Dead.

Winter Wings

When surrendering the
Insatiable hunger for death,
A fullness of life is aroused as the sun
Bursts forth from the clouded horizon.
And the Spirit descends displaying
The pluming fullness of glory,
Lying to rest on still waters
In the presence of grateful hearts.

Invitation

Redemption
Is an invitation,
Not a location.

Surrender
Expectation; enter
Merely a lover

Engaging
With another, bringing
Hope anew. Breathing

In the night,
The longing two souls might
Experience light

And nearness.
So unite and express
Simple sacredness.

Naked. Near.
Of one flesh. Feel. See. Hear.
Worship. Fullness. Tears.

Night Ornaments

As day fades to dusk
    and shadow descends,
The fireflies come forth
Exalting with flame.
Ornamenting hazed leaves

Dusk drowns to darkness.
Leaves submerged in to night.
The fire shines brighter,
Resounding the light.
Ornamenting lost life.

Time ceases existing.
Hope's concealed with'n black.
When all seems to vanish
    the fireflies have stayed.
Ornamenting veiled lies.

I

When the winds rage forth,
Driving me back in force,
Am I only chaff being blown away?

When the winds calm still,
And all seems absent of thrill,
To where does my mind meditate?

You have rooted me deep,
The Good Gardener of my soul.
A tree planted for good fruit and leaf.
In the streams of your love I stand whole.
With tender care you've sowed and you reap.

II

What is the strength of the Lord?
And what is it to fear Him rightly?
Do I rejoice with trembling too lightly?
And reject fear on my own accord?

I never see you as an angry son,
Is your anger solely for the vain?
In knowing your anger what have I to gain?
O come Lord Jesus, come!

III

When fleeing from the darkness,
Pain is ready to inject.
Salvation seems a distant hope,
And my soul my own to protect.   (Selah)

My glory broke, my head hung low,
This sorrow I long to forget.
But in this place of broken rest,
My salvation stands erect.   (Selah)

Surround me, my Shield, in your strength,
Breathe hope in to this wretch.
You lift the head that's been brought low,
"Selah, my son, take rest."
                                                  (Selah)

Just Man

To enter in to any
Is to surrender.
A giving of yourself
Of faith, hope, fear.

It is true one can
Move forward without a step
Of surrender. Yet this is
Not how to enter, but merely exist.

To enter in is to give,
And give, and give. In hope.
The return is fear, and hurt,
But not alone and not always.

No, not always and not ever alone,
For in every step we are love.
And love cries forth, "fear not,
Dear child" as fear draws near.

In fear love is able
And near, as we enter again,
And again, and again. So I plea
Make me soft, let me breathe.

I long to more than exist, more
Than be. I long to step forth,
To speak light, to awaken from sleep.
To fearfully and faithfully
    Surrender into intimacy.

FUNgi

Mushrooms
Springing Forth
Playful Little Heirlooms
Of Land and Nature's Abounding Worth
Your Presence, A Reminder, Redemption is Rife!
Cap
Spore
Life

The Search
Surveying the Depths
Amidst Elm, Oak and Birch
Provision Sought as the Land Provideths
Alas! You've Been Spotted, Death and Life's Allegory
Found
Picked
Glory

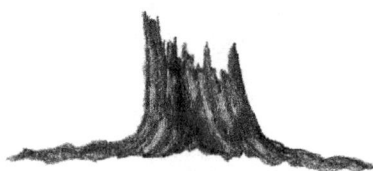

To Be Seen

Is it a good thing
    To be seen?

It seems to me
    Most of the beheld
    Have been beaten, berated, banished or broken.

Is being seen only
    The first step to suppression?

What corruption lies beneath the eye!
Limitless destruction of beauty. Profanity.
    Danger in every sunrise.

It seems to me
    If existence has shown us anything,
    To be deeply hidden is the only place to be free.
    Lest pain be our ceaseless reality.

Control possessed to cease existing;
    It is a mirage; an apparition.
    We are always seen; seeing; succumbing.

The real question is never the
    First question.
It always lies silent within.
The real question is
    Do we see ourselves only in
    The eyes of the seer?

For it is so very difficult to find stillness
In the mind of another.

Selah, Dear Sparrow

The sprightly sparrow,
Darting to and fro.
Constantly in motion.
Always alert and on guard.
Searching and seeking
Without end.
Restless in spirit.
Where is your solace?
Is not your lot
One of never-ceasing exertion?
Yet even you, dear sparrow,
Constant in motion,
Can find rest everlasting,
In the home of your Creator.

So often my heart, darts
To and fro as sister sparrow.
Searching for hope,
Solace, inspiration.
And like my dear friend
Who nests in the Father's presence,
My soul too finds rest,
In the courts of my dear Saviour.

To my Bride:
(I love every dance we share together)

The sun has descended.
A billion stars watch enviously from the sky.
The moon our brilliant spotlight.
The breeze a curtain blowing in the night.
Our hearts are the drumbeat,
Our whispers the enchanting lyrics.
We hold each other ever so tightly,
Longing never to let go.
Our love is the music,
The most beautiful of melodies.
The dance is the presence,
Of God's love flowing through us.
In your arms I am happy.
In your arms I feel whole.
In your arms I come alive,
As we dance to the music of our souls.

www.ingramcontent.com/pod-product-compliance
Lightning Source LLC
Chambersburg PA
CBHW031223090426
42740CB00007B/686